Francisco Pizarro & The Inca: The Culture and Conquest of the Inca Empire

By Charles River Editors

Sacsayhuamán, the Inca stronghold of Cusco

About Charles River Editors

Charles River Editors was founded by Harvard and MIT alumni to provide superior editing and original writing services, with the expertise to create digital content for publishers across a vast range of subject matter. In addition to providing original digital content for third party publishers, Charles River Editors republishes civilization's greatest literary works, bringing them to a new generation via ebooks.

Introduction

Banner of the Inca

During the Age of Exploration, Native American tribes fell victim to European conquerors seeking legendary cities made of gold and other riches, attempts that were often being made in vain. And yet, of all the empires that were conquered across the continent, the one that continues to be most intimately associated with legends of gold and hidden riches is the Inca Empire. The Inca Empire, which flourished in modern day Peru and along the west coast of South America, was the largest Native American empire in pre-Columbian America until Pizarro and the Spanish conquistadors conquered them in the 16th century. What ultimately sealed their doom was the rumor that huge amounts of gold were available in regions south of the Andes Mountains.

Though the Spanish physically conquered them in quick fashion, the culture and legacy of the Inca Empire has continued to endure throughout the centuries in both Europe and South America, due in no small part to the fact they were one of the most advanced and sophisticated cultures on the continent. Like the Aztecs, the Spanish burned much of the Inca's extant writings, but it is estimated that as many as 35 million once fell under their banner, and the empire's administrative skills were so sharp that they kept accurate census records. Their religion, organization, and laws were also effectively centralized and tied to the rulers of the empire, and their military mobilization would have made the ancient Spartans proud. After the Spanish conquest, several rebellions in the area attempted to reestablish the proud Inca Empire over the next two centuries, all while famous Europeans like Voltaire glorified the Inca Empire in optimistic artistic portrayals.

The mystique and aura of the Inca continue to fascinate the world today, and nowhere is this more prominent than at Macchu Picchu, which was "lost" for over 300 years and remains the subject of intense debate among historians. The magnificent ruins and the inability of historians to crack the code used for the Inca's few surviving written records all continue to add to the mystery and interest in the Inca civilization.

Francisco Pizarro & The Inca comprehensively covers the culture and history of pre-Columbian America's largest empire. Along with pictures of Inca art, clothing and ruins, this book describes the Inca's lives, religion, cities, and empire, in an attempt to better understand the once dominant but still mysterious civilization.

Francisco Pizarro González (circa 1471/6-1541)

"Friends and comrades! On that side [south] are toil, hunger, nakedness, the drenching storm, desertion, and death; on this side ease and pleasure. There lies Peru with its riches; here, Panama and its poverty. Choose, each man, what best becomes a brave Castilian. For my part, I go to the south." – Francisco Pizarro

During the Age of Exploration, some of the most famous and infamous individuals were Spain's best known conquistadors. Naturally, as one of the best known conquistadors, Francisco Pizarro (1471/6-1541) is also one of the most controversial. Like Christopher Columbus and Hernan Cortés before him, Pizarro was celebrated in Europe for subduing the Inca Empire, a culture that fascinated his contemporaries. At the same time, naturally, indigenous views of the man have been overwhelmingly negative.

If Columbus and Cortés were the pioneers of Spain's new global empire, Pizarro consolidated its immense power and riches, and his successes inspired a further generation to expand Spain's dominions to unheard of dimensions. Furthermore, he participated in the forging of a new culture: like Cortés, he took an indigenous mistress with whom he had two mixed-race children, and yet the woman has none of the lasting fame of Cortés's Doña Marina. With all of this in mind, it is again remarkable that Pizarro remains one of the less well-known and less written about of the explorers of his age.

On the other hand, there are certain factors that may account for the conqueror of Peru's relative lack of lasting glory. For one, he was a latecomer in more than one sense. Cortés's reputation was built on being the first to overthrow a great empire, so Pizarro's similar feat, even if it bore even greater fruit in the long run, would always be overshadowed by his predecessor's precedent. But Pizarro also lacked the youthful glamour of Cortés: already a wizened veteran in his 50s by the time he undertook his momentous expedition, he proceeded with the gritty determination of a hardened soldier rather than the audacity and cunning of a young courtier.

Francisco Pizarro & The Inca chronicles Pizarro's life, but it also examines the aftermath of his conquest and analyzes the controversy surrounding his legacy. Along with pictures of important people, places, and events in his life, you will learn about Pizarro like you never have before, in no time at all.

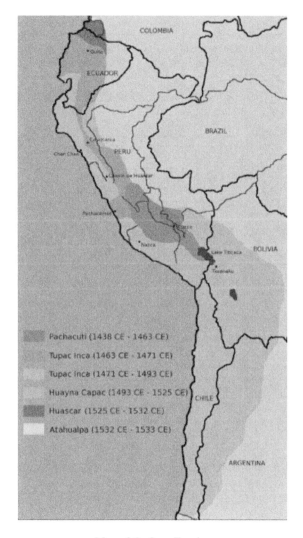

Map of the Inca Empire

Chapter 1 History of the Incas

According to history as created by Inca oral tradition, preserved by memory keepers and written down by Spanish commentators after the conquest, there was no culture or civilization in

Peru before the Incas arrived on the scene. Given these origins, anthropologists speculate that in the interest of ensuring their dominance in the area, the Incas purposely extinguished any local histories that existed in their empire, so that for all the peoples of the empire history began when the Incas appeared. Ironically, this was accomplished in much the same way and with similar results as the Spanish attempt to destroy the Incas' own memory of their history and civilization.

Precursors of the Incas

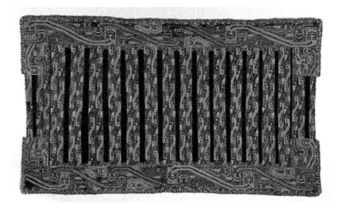

Paracas Mantle, Los Angeles County Museum of Art

The Inca people, in spite of their own propaganda or manipulated oral history, did not suddenly appear in a cultureless environment. In fact, people dwelt in the Inca lands as early as 3000 B.C., and archaeologists working at various sites have found pottery and textiles that indicate a rich history of pre-Inca Andean cultures. Among these is the Paracas culture, named by archaeologists after the Paracas Peninsula, where a rich deposit of finely woven textiles was found in shaft burials. The Paracas culture, which existed from 800-100 B.C., was based on irrigated agriculture.

Another pre-Inca culture of the region was the Moche civilization, which flourished on the coastal region of northern Peru from about 100-800 A.D. The Moche were expert builders, as the remains of their adobe temples near Huaca de la Luna testify. And around the same time the Moche were constructing their cities, the Nazca culture rose on the southern coast of Peru. It was the Nazca who etched the mysterious lines in the desert gravel around 500 A.D. that have been interpreted by UFO-ologists and New Agers to be sophisticated Martian landing strips.

One of the most advanced pre-Inca cultures was the Tiwanaku. The remains of this culture, which was centered in northern Bolivia, indicate that it was based on sophisticated agricultural practices with terraced fields and irrigated lowlands, and that it expanded its influence through widespread conquest.

Tiwanaku Vase, Tiwanaka Museum, La Paz, Bolivia Photo: Christophe Meneboeuf

It was into this rich cultural environment that the Incas inserted their own social organization and became dominant through wars of expansion and, it is assumed, astute bureaucratic control.

The Inca Story of Their Origin

The Inca myth of their origin was kept alive and modified according to their needs through oral history. They believed that their ancestors came from Pacariqtambo, about 21 miles from modern Cuzco. Here there were three caves. From the central cave came four brothers and four sisters, and from the side caves streamed the people who were to be the ancestors of all the clans of the Incas.

This group then set off to find a permanent home, but among these original leaders, only Ayar Manco of the brothers survived. The four sisters were more fortunate and all lived to help establish the first Inca city. One of the sisters, Mama Huaca, delivered Ayar Manco's son, who was called Sinchi Roca. When the migrating clans arrived in the valley of Cuzco, Mama Huaca proved herself to be a ferocious combatant against the people that the Incas found there. Using her bola (Spanish) or as it was called by the Inca, ayllo, she captured one of the enemy soldiers and ripped out his lungs and squeezed them until they exploded, thus causing the enemy to flee. Ayar Manco, or as he styled himself, Manco Cápac, and his sisters then built houses in the valley and established a town for the three original, Inca lineages.

Later History of the Inca

At Cuzco the Incas thrived under a series of rulers and under the protection of the sun god, for whom they built a temple. In the 13th century, the 8th Inca leader, Virachocha Inca, assumed the title of Sapa Inca, or unique, supreme leader. It was under his rule that the Incas began the creation of their empire by dominating the highlands around Cuzco and subjugating temporarily the Chanca people in the south of modern Peru.

In 1438, the Incas continued expanding their sphere of influence under the leadership of Pachacúti Inca Yupanqui, who after his initial conquest (or possibly re-conquest) of the Chanca placed the Inca warriors under his brother Capac Yupanqui. Unfortunately, Capac Yupanqui was unsuccessful in chasing down and slaughtering all the Chanca and was punished for his failure by forfeiting his life.

The next great expansion of the Inca Empire took place under Túpac Inca Yupanqui. As a prince commander he extended the Inca Empire north into modern Ecuador, where he rebuilt the city of Quito. After ascending to the throne in about 1471, according to a Spanish commentator, he sailed out to some islands in the Pacific, which may have been the Galapagos and Easter Island, ultimately returning to Cuzco with black people, gold and a chair of brass. This may be an entirely mythic voyage, but it is a fact that Túpac Inca Yupanqui was successful in pushing the frontiers of empire north into Ecuador and south into Chile.

The son of Túpac Inca Yupanqui was Huyana Capac who expanded the Inca Empire into Argentina and further into Chile. The Empire was now at its greatest extent, stretching over vast tracts of land in modern day Bolivia, Ecuador, Columbia, Peru, Chile and Argentina. It is thought that Huyana Capac died of smallpox, which by now was spreading rapidly from Spanish dominated Central America. It was Huyana Capac's two sons, Húascar and Atahualpa, who became engaged in civil war just prior to the arrival of the Spanish.

Chapter 2: Religion of the Incas

Although the Inca's oral traditions suggested that the history of the region began with their empire, the various gods and the religious ceremonies of the peoples that inhabited the Inca's lands before their arrival were assimilated into the Inca Empire and were incorporated into Inca religion. However, under Inca rule, all those gods were to be subordinate to those gods of the Incas themselves, so as to ensure that Imperial authority was clear and without dispute among all quarters of the Empire.

Viracocha was the primary god in the Inca pantheon. He was the origin and creator of all things. His son, the god Inti, or the sun, was married to Mama Quilla, the moon, who was also created by Viracocha. According to one myth, Inti was the father of Manco Cápac, the founder of the Inca ruling dynasty, but it was believed by some that Viracocha himself fathered Manco Cápac. In practice, the Inca centered their religious worship on Inti, and this god's High Priest was the second most important person in Inca society. The god Inti was honored at an annual celebration held each June. The Inti Raymi festival included sacrifices, feasts and sexual abstinence.

Inti, or the Sun God. Design for a flag of Peru designed by José Bernardo de Tagle, 1822

The Inca cosmology was imposed throughout the Empire, and temples to the Sun were constructed and staffed by religious officials who were allotted farmland called 'lands of the Sun'. Other local cults were provided with produce from these lands as well.

The main temple of Inca religion was the Coricancha or Sun Temple in Cuzco, in which was kept the great golden disk of the sun. The disk was appropriated by the Spanish in 1571 and sent off to the Pope. While it has disappeared, perhaps lost somewhere during the tortuous route to Spain, it remains alive in the fabulous world of adventure story writers, New Age mystics and manufacturers of souvenirs. It became a major element in the iconography of the 19th century independence movement in South America, as a symbol of nations freed from the yoke of the Spanish crown.

Two other gold images were installed in the Coricancha by Pachacúti Inca in the 15th century. One was called Viracocha Pachayachachi, which represented the creator of everything, and the other, Chuqui ylla, represented the God of Thunder. It was to Thunder that the Incas addressed their petitions for water, and shrines to him were built around the Empire, some surviving to this day in the highlands where his worship was associated with the morning star, Venus.

The moon goddess, Mama Quilla, was connected with the ruler's consort. She regulated the months and the calendar and, as such, was an important element in the creation of the Inca calendar of festivals. Her shrines were ornamented in silver and managed by priestesses.

Another female deity was Pachamama or Mother Earth. Her special interest was agriculture, and she too was of particular importance in the domain of the ruler's consort.

Chapter 3: Everyday Life among the Incas

The Incas spoke a language they called runasimi, and which the conquistadors called quechua. Quechua was introduced in the Inca culture after 1338, so it is assumed that they had another language prior to settling in Cuzco. It is also believed that the elite may have continued to use this original language. Quechua, which has eight figures of speech, no articles, no gender and a small vocabulary, was imposed as the *lingua franca* by the Incas in their empire to facilitate communication between many different cultural groups that fell under Inca administration.

The group of indigenous Andeans that established themselves as the Incas at Cuzco developed a culture that was in some ways unique and in other ways similar to that of other indigenous Andean peoples. Like all good imperialists, the Inca were expert assimilationists, making it often difficult to determine with certainty what the Inca inherited from earlier cultures and what was unique to them. For example, many of the basic ideas in their building projects had reached particularly high levels of development before the Incas employed them. Vertical archipelago agriculture practiced by the Incas, in which terraced fields were layered on mountainsides, and the construction of bridges, roads and irrigation canals, were common in Andean cultures long before the rise of the Incas.

Vertical Archipelago Agriculture, Choquequirao Peru

The Incas, however, seem to have taken the management of water to a new level of sophistication. Because cleanliness was of importance to the members of the ruling class, they included sunken baths, with hot and cold water, in their palaces. For those of minor rank in Cuzco, there were public baths in the form of fountains beside the main streets.

Given this sophistication, it is no surprise that the majority of Incas were farmers who tilled land granted to them by the ruler of the Inca state. In return for the land, the Inca farmer was required to contribute his labor to public works, and surplus food was contributed to supply the elite. The system of taxes in kind or labor was called mit'a, and it was at the very centre of the Inca social system. Of course, this arrangement was nearly identical to European feudalism of the same time period, and as it turned out, the Spanish would largely leave the mit'a system in place after conquering the Inca Empire.

Inca Clothing

Inca Tunic, Dumbarton Oaks, Washington

The nobility had a large wardrobe and changed their clothes after bathing. The males wore simple garments of rectangles of woven, naturally died alpaca or vicuña wool, which was sewn together and tied by a knot or pin. Clothes were standardized, and rank was denoted by headwear and style of hair, which was cut with obsidian knives. Sandals had soles of Llama leather and were fastened with braided cords.

Inca women's clothes were a little more complicated than those worn by the men. A long shift of two rectangles of cloth was cinched at the waist by a belt, and a second mantle which fell from shoulders to feet, closed by pins of gold and silver, was worn over it.

Both the male and female members of the nobility wore jewelry, but most was worn by men. Cylindrical ear-plugs of gold or wood were worn by the men of the royal lineage, the elite wore necklaces with metal disks, and the highest level of the aristocracy decorated themselves with wide gold and silver bracelets. Feathers were frequently used for ornamentation.

Diet

The Inca diet was very basic, consisting mostly of maize, potatoes and qunoa, while the little meat that was consumed consisted of guinea pig. All the dishes were prepared by boiling or roasting in clay ovens, since their ceramic cooking vessels were not suitable for frying.

The Inca elite seem to have supplemented their diet with some game and even fish that were brought in from the coast by runners. The drink consumed by all classes was chichi, a concoction made by chewing quinoa, maize or mollberries and spitting it into warm water, where it fermented. Very simple drinking vessels, called qero, made from wood or pottery, was used for the beverage, which was consumed in quantity at banquets and religious festivals.

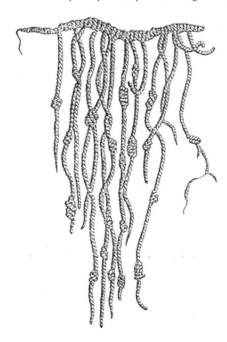

It is widely believed that Inca festivals were venues where the tales of the history of the people were retold by a special group of the elite who were responsible for keeping Imperial history. The oral records of the Inca, who had no writing, were memorized and repeated with the assistance of quipu or knotted colored cords. How exactly the quipu functioned is unknown, but it is assumed that the knots provided numerical information, which may have been in a decimal system that was decipherable by quipucamayocs or keepers of the quipus. Given their limited language and lack of writing, it's astounding that the Inca Empire was as well organized and expansive as it was, and it seems that its success can be attributed to the quipus, which were used not only for history but also for the details of administration of the empire. Amazingly, quantities of quipus found in burial sites have provided modern archaeologists and cryptographers with a puzzle which has, in spite of the application of modern code-solving techniques, yet to be solved.

As well as the recitation of history, the festivals included the presentation of drama, the singing of hymns, and the presentation of narrative poems. The hymns of Pachacuti Inca Yupanqui are among the great works of sacred poetry. One of them runs;

O Creator, root of all,

Wiracocha, end of all,

Lord in shining garments

Who infuses life

And sets all things in order,

Saying,

"Let there be man!

Let there ber woman

Molder, maker,

To all things you have given life:

Watch over them,

Keep them living prosperously,

Fortunately,

In safety and peace.

The festival actors who presented stories of heroic exploits, wars and greatness of the Incas were members of the elite - nobles, imperial administrators and priests. It is possible that the plays were accompanied by dances and music, which would have been produced by simple instruments such as flutes, drums, panpipes and conch shell horns.

Chapter 4: The Inca Empire

The Inca referred to their own empire as *Tawantinsuyu*, which meant "fourt parts together" in their language. This is because the Inca Empire was administered as four provincial departments: Chinchasuyu (NW), Antiwuyu (NE), Kuntisuyu (SW), and Qullasuyu (SE). These *Tawantinsuyu* or four regions or the four united provinces were connected to Cuzco by roads along which runners could pass quickly to deliver information from the court of the ruler to provincial governors and vice versa. The roads also allowed the quick movement of warriors to any part of the empire where they were needed, and it accomodated the large parties of those rendering mit'a or labor to make their way to construction sites, which were especially numerous in the last years of the empire.

The extent of the Inca road system is evidence of its importance in the economy and administration of the Empire. The backbone of the system of communication was the Qhapaq Ñan, which ran 3,700 miles along the length of the Andes, connecting Santiago to Quito. Many other roads allowed for the quick negotiation of the often very mountainous terrain of the empire, which encompassed a large part of western South America from southern Ecuador and Columbia and western Bolivia to northwest Argentina, and central Chile. It is estimated that the network of Inca roads totaled some 24,000 miles. With that said, the use of the word "road" is a bit of a misnomer, because the Inca had no wheeled vehicles and no pack animals. Since they always moved on foot, certain stretches of a road could more aptly be described as a narrow path.

The Imperial population connected by the road system is estimated to have been anywhere from 4 to 37 million. It is presumed that many of the quipu that have been preserved up to the present day are census records, but in the absence of a key to their code it is not possible to know with any degree of accuracy the population of the Inca Empire.

The Inca ruler, who claimed direct descent from the sun through the founder Manco Capac, considered the people of the empire his sons and all the women his spouses. His authority was spread throughout the empire by his court of elite nobles who received their power by direct connection to the ruler through royal blood.

The Inca developed a sophisticated system of imperial administration that is not yet completely understood. In the conquered territories, they apparently used the heads of the leading local families as administrators. These chiefs were called *curaca* under the Incas, and the office was hereditary. At the same time, these local administrators were not to call themselves Incas and were clearly kept in a subservient position to the elite of Cuzco. The *curaca* were responsible for ensuring that appropriate tribute was forwarded to the Inca Emperor, mainly in the form of mit'a or labor. To ensure that Imperial authority remained consistent, the children of the *curaca* were sent to Cuzco to be taught Inca administrative systems.

Not much is known about the Inca system of law and its application to the conquered territories. Presumably there were local courts that enforced edicts from Cuzco and ensured that surpluses in agricultural produce were stored and forwarded to the elite when demanded.

Chapter 5: Inca Architecture

An Inca Wall, Cuzco

Nearly 500 years after the Spanish conquest, travellers to Peru and neighboring countries that formed the Inca Empire are still amazed by the unequalled skill of Inca masons. This includes modern tourists, 19th century explorers like Hiram Bingham (the discoverer of Machu Picchu in 1911), and the Spanish conquistadors and colonial settlers.

Once again, the success of Inca architecture was a byproduct of their ability to assimilate the work and techniques of past cultures. The exacting masonry of Inca municipal buildings, paved roads, bridges, irrigation canals and agricultural terraces was not unprecedented in the region. The Incas assimilated and developed techniques of art and architecture that were already practiced in the cultures that they conquered and incorporated into their Empire.

Gate of the Sun, Tiwanaku, Bolivia

The Inca ruler Packakuti Inca Yupanqui, in his expansionist conquests, defeated the people of Tiwanaku in western Bolivia around 1450. The city he vanquished was a substantial one in which the buildings were constructed of precisely cut stone, smoothly polished and assembled in interlocking courses or layers. Tiwanaku was not a minor country outpost; archaeologists and historians speculate it may have had upwards of 285,000-1,500,000 inhabitants and controlled a large empire that it had apparently acquired over several centuries.

Walls of The Temple Kalasasaya, Tiwanaku, Bolivia. Photo: Anakin

Pakakuti was certainly impressed by the substantial glory of Tiwanaku, and as part of the tribute mit'a, he took masons to Cuzco and set them to work transforming the inferior adobe village into a highly organized symbol of power, constructed with stone. The new city was planned on the shape of a puma, which was inserted between the two rivers Huatanay and Tullumayo. Canals were then built with masonry walls to protect the city from flooding. A grid plan with narrow streets was established and plazas were laid out, with the city's blocks lined with kancha or compounds of buildings surrounded by masonry walls. The city at its greatest extent housed more than 40,000 inhabitants, and with suburban settlements was estimated by a commentator in 1553 to have had a population of 200,000.

At one end of the city - the puma's tail - was the Coricancha or Temple of the Sun. It must have been quite a sight, even if one discounts the Spanish chroniclers' propensity for exaggeration. The magnificence of this enclosed religious precinct served as a powerful symbol of Inca Imperial authority, and it was said that the Coricancha had walls and floors covered with sheets of gold and that the adjoining courtyard was full of golden statues. Unfortunately, the temple and its splendor naturally became the focus of Spanish attempts to abolish idolatry in their new empire, leading the new rulers to strip the Temple of its gold leaf interior and melt down the golden statues. Eventually, the Temple itself was levelled and replaced by the Church of Santo Domingo.

Inca Masonry Photo: Hakan Svensson

Two grand municipal plazas were laid out in the middle of Cuzco. One of these, Haucaypata Plaza, was surrounded with buildings of symbolic importance, including the temples and great halls for ceremonial and administrative gatherings.

The doorways of all these buildings were trapezoidal and had double stepped jambs. This particular architectural motif became so ubiquitous in Inca building that it appeared throughout the Empire as a symbol of the dominance of the Incas of Cuzco.

Typical Inca Doorway Ollantaytambo Photo Stevage

The administration of the Inca Empire was such that the forms of buildings and town planning established at Cuzco in the 1450's was repeated in a standardized form in building campaigns elsewhere up until the Spanish conquest. This was not unlike the municipal building programs that the British would establish through their empire. The idea that Cuzco was the center of an Empire that was comprised of four provinces was manifest in the planning of the city, where there was a central intersection of the four roads that led to the four divisions of the Empire.

Granaries or houses on hillside at Ollantaytambo

Archaeologists have studied a number of cities and towns built by the Inca's in various reaches of the Empire. In the Peruvian town of Ollantaytambo, the Incas repeated their grid plan in organizing the urban architecture, even though it stretches over uneven ground. They also repeated the form of building that was developed at Cuzco, with large and small rectangular spaces of a single story roofed with thatch supported on a wooden framework. This town, unfinished at the time of the Spanish conquest, was linked to Machu Picchu by a stone paved road. On a steep mountainside adjacent to the city there are remains of several houses or grain storage chambers clustered together. The rectangular rooms would have been covered by thatched roofs supported on a ridge pole running between the stone gabled ends.

Machu Picchu

Machu Picchu, now the best known of Inca urban centers, is a fortified city whose function in Inca civilization is still not clear. Some have speculated that it was an outpost or a frontier citadel, while others believe it to be a sanctuary or a work center for women. Still others suggest that it was a ceremonial center or perhaps even the last refuge of the Incas after the conquest. One of the theories that has taken hold is that Macchu Picchu was the summer dwelling of the Inca's royal court, the Inca's version of Versailles. As was the case with the renaming of Mayan and Aztec ruins, the names given to various structures by archaeologists are purely imaginary and thus not very helpful; for example, the mausoleum, palace or watchtower may have been nothing of the sort.

Machu Picchu Photo: Martin St.-Amant

What is clear at Machu Picchu is that the urban plan and the building techniques employed followed those at Cuzco. The location of plazas and the clever use of the irregularities in the land, along with the highly developed aesthetic involved in masonry work, follow the model of the Inca capital. The typical Incan technique of meticulous assembling ashlar masonry and creating walls of blocks without a binding material is astounding. The blocks are sometimes evenly squared and sometimes are of varying shape. In the latter case, the very tight connection between the blocks of stone seems quite remarkable. Even more astounding than the precise stone cutting of the Incas is the method that they used for the transportation and movement on site of these enormous blocks. The Incas did not have the wheel, so all the work was accomplished using rollers and levers.

The Incas did not develop a way of creating vaults of stone, so all of their structures are thus based on simple two-dimensional geometry. Because the architectural repertoire of the Incas did not include the arch or the vault, their buildings are all one story in height, the doorways and windows are headed by flat stones and are thus limited in breadth, and the ceilings are the underside of the thatched roofs.

In all the Inca cities there were one or more kallankas or great halls. The function of these buildings is still not clear. They may have been used for festivals, audiences with administrators, barracks for soldiers or council houses. One of the greatest of these kallankas is to be found at Puno, Peru. Here the Raqchi or so-called Temple of the Wiraqocha is a great rectangular long hall that had a roof supported by a series of 11 pillars along each side of a central dividing wall which itself was penetrated by 10 doorways. 15 doorways opened to the main plaza. The walls of this structure, which measure about 300 feet in length and 80 feet in breadth, were constructed in adobe set on a stone base wall.

The So-called Temple of Wiraqocha at Puno, Peru

Chapter 6: Pizarro's Origins and Early Career

Like Hernán Cortés and many other members of the front line of Spanish imperial expansion, Francisco Pizarro was born in the southwestern Spanish province of Extremadura. It was more or less the closest region geographically to the Indies, and due to its proximity to the great ports of Seville, Cádiz, and Lisbon, it had a more maritime and Atlantic orientation than the northern and eastern regions of Spain, which tended to look more to Europe and the Mediterranean. It was also a bone-dry and economically marginal region of greater than average poverty, where the experience of long-term war with the Moors and with Mediterranean rivals had created a frontier-like mentality and helped form a large class of men who sought their fortune in war rather than in commerce, the church, or courtly activity.

Francisco's father, Gonzalo Pizarro, belonged to this class and was an infantry officer with a relatively prestigious lineage who fought in a number of Mediterranean campaigns. His mother, on the other hand, was a poor woman who bore her son out of wedlock and later married another man, with whom she had several other sons. In part because of the humble circumstances of his birth and in part because of the general scarcity of birth records from the period, it is not clear

Statue of Balboa in Madrid

Balboa would join the pantheon of conquistadors, though he is not remembered today for conquering anything. Balboa was, however, the first European to see the Pacific Ocean from the New World. Since it was the Pacific Ocean that Columbus originally sought to reach, this was a pivotal moment in the exploration and conquest of the Americas. Not coincidentally, Balboa reached the Pacific by crossing over the narrow piece of land that would one day become Panama, and which to this day serves via the Panama Canal as a crucial East-West conduit for trade. It was with Balboa that Panama first became a major geopolitical hotspot, not least because it was from there that Pizarro launched his missions down the western coast of South America. But prior to setting off across the isthmus, Balboa had established the city of Santa

María del Darién, where both he and Pizarro established themselves as leading colonists.

Despite his accomplishments, Balboa was not appointed governor of the new settlement, and the position was instead given to Pedrarias Dávila, a veteran soldier of aristocratic background with close ties to the crown. A rivalry developed between the two men, and their conflict culminated in Dávila's execution of Balboa in 1519. By this point, Pizarro had established close ties with Dávila and had conspired against his former comrade Balboa. In exchange for his loyalty, Pizarro ascended in position, becoming mayor of Panama City and gaining a valuable land grant.

Despite his modest success in the new colony, Pizarro clearly had his eyes on a bigger prize, and this fact is not terribly surprising: Panama was in a backwater area that had not yielded the wealth in gold and other precious items that had been anticipated. And while the Pacific had been reached, Asia was still a long way away.

On the other hand, the Spaniards now had reliable informants among the local natives, and it was from them that they heard rumors of a great kingdom to the South, named Virú or Birú, a place of fabulous wealth and abundance. In the meantime, by the early 1520s the settlers of Panama had heard news of Cortés's conquest to the north, a development that certainly raised their hopes and likely inspired their envy. Perhaps most importantly, there was now a propitious environment for an adventurous man to raise up an expedition, men eager to take part, and financiers willing to cover the costs of equipping several ships and several hundred men with the necessary supplies and weapons for a trip of uncertain duration and results. In Diego de Almagro, another Spaniard of humble origins settled in Panama, Pizarro found a partner and collaborator. The two signed a contract on a joint venture to the south in 1524 and promised to divide all eventual proceeds between them. The relationship with Almagro would be a crucial one for the rest of Pizarro's life, and would end up being a pivotal factor in his death.

19th century painting of Diego de Almagro

By the time Pizarro and Almagro began preparing their first venture down the Pacific coast, they had been preceded by Pascal de Anadagoya, an explorer of Basque origin. Andagoya's 1522 excursion had failed as a mission of conquest because of hostility from the natives on the coast and poor weather, but his returning crew had brought back persuasive evidence of the existence of a great and wealthy empire to the south. It was now only a matter of time before other would-be conquistadors took up the challenge, so Pizarro and Almagro hurriedly assembled a small expeditionary force of about 80,and managed to obtain permission from Dávila, to whom they and any lands they managed to conquer would remain subordinate.

Depiction of Davila

Pizarro set out late in September 1524, while Almagro stayed behind with the intention of recruiting more men and catching up with the forward party. As it turned out, the mission was for the most part a disaster. Like Andagoya and his men before them, the Spaniards under Pizarro's command were met with relentless hostility from the natives on the shore, and poor weather and limited supplies made things even worse. In the end, the entire force returned in early 1525 with little to show for their efforts.

What they had seen, though, evidently confirmed the rich rewards of conquest if it was achieved, and so they set out again in August of 1526, this time with a force about twice as large as the first expedition's. As in their own previous expedition and Andagoya's, they met with hostility all along the coast of what are now Colombia and Ecuador, and their attempts to establish footholds on the land and explore the interior bore little fruit. The conditions were so poor and the palpable rewards so scarce that by 1527, many of the men preferred to return to Panama, where they went with Almagro when he returned to gather supplies and recruit replacements.

Meanwhile, Pizarro and a small group pressed on, and the results were finally encouraging. They reached Tumbes, a coastal city at the edge of the Incan domains. They were impressed with the more "civilized" appearance of the settlement and with the great quantities of gold and silver belonging to the local *cacique*, a tributary of the Incas, and they were generally treated in a friendly way by the inhabitants. One of them, a young boy, accepted baptism and later returned with Pizarro to Panama. Felipillo, as he came to be called by the Spaniards, would become their principal translator in their engagements with the Inca emperor and his emissaries in future years.

On the strength of the solid evidence of wealth that he brought back from Tumbes, Pizarro returned to Spain in 1528 – he had not been back in 20 years – to seek permission from the crown to undertake the conquest of Peru. This way, he would be able to operate independently rather than under the command of the governor of Panama, and even more importantly he would have access to a larger share of all proceeds. Probably encouraged by the recent success of Cortés and himself desperate for new sources of revenue, Charles V was receptive to Pizarro's solicitation and in the end granted him the licence or *capitulación* necessary to undertake the conquest. On the strength of this political coup and his promises of great wealth, Pizarro was able to recruit a large force of men from his native Extremadura, including his four half-brothers. Back in Panama, meanwhile, Almagro was assembling more participants, while the priest Hernando de Luque, a third partner, gathered funds from investors.

Charles V

While the capitulación was probably Pizarro's most impressive accomplishment thus far, it had the side effect of creating tension between him and Almagro, a tension that would continue to build and have a decisive influence on both men's fates. Upon Pizarro's return to Panama, Almagro was unhappy with what seemed to him the unfair and unequal division of the rewards of conquest determined by the king. Pizarro was to be Governor and Captain General of Peru (the same position won by Cortés in Mexico), while Almagro obtained the far less glorious concession of the governorship of Tumbes. Furthermore, the presence of a large contingent of Pizarro's family appeared to Almagro an affront to their supposed partnership, since he rightly surmised that Pizarro would be inclined to hand out lucrative rewards to his brothers. While the nascent conflict did not derail the preparations in any serious ways, Almagro's resentments would now be left to simmer beneath the surface, and it would only be a matter of time before they would explode.

Chapter 7: The Conquest of the Inca Empire

The Inca Empire may have consisted of 4 parts, but the unity was quite fragile, as the empire had only existed in its current state for about a century when Pizarro arrived. Brought together by a combination of military conquests and peaceful takeovers involving royal intermarriage, a combination of tribute, trade, and centralized administration held the various territories under Inca rule together, even as they remained politically and culturally relatively autonomous. Still, the first Spaniards to see Peru commented on the orderliness of their system of government and the impressive productivity of their agriculture, which produced grain surpluses stored in a network of warehouses and distributed during drought years. With some more recalcitrant conquered groups, the rulers had undertaken forced resettlements and practical enslavement, but for the most part, Inca rule had been peaceful and prosperous for some time. The war between Huascar and Atahualpa had introduced a disorienting period of political chaos and conflicted loyalties that would be initially exploited and then seriously exacerbated by the newly arrived Spaniards.

After months of gathering the latest intelligence, Pizarro determined that Atahualpa had gained a decisive advantage in the conflict and that his troops had taken Huascar captive in the capital of Cuzco. Having been based in the north, Atahualpa was now marching south with a large army toward Cuzco. Pizarro, with fewer than 200 men, decided to go for broke against a far superior force, in the hope of striking a dramatic blow against the Incas. Probably inspired by Cortés's strategy in Mexico, which involved the capture of Moctezuma for ransom, he hatched the plan of leading Atahualpa into a trap and taking him hostage. The plans for the trap were probably also borrowed from Cortés and his lieutenant Pedro de Alvarado, who first in the city of Cholula and then in the Aztec capital of Tenochtitlán managed to ambush thousands of indigenous nobles and warriors by cornering them in confined spaces and attacking them by surprise.

16th century depiction of Atahualpa

The enterprise was an enormous gamble premised entirely on treachery and unprovoked violence, and even if it succeeded, there was no guarantee that it would lead to ultimate victory. Even though Almagro might show up with a larger force of several hundred, Atahualpa had perhaps as many as 10,000 in his immediate retinue and was supported by several armies of more than 30,000. The terrain was mountainous, climactically variable, and completely unknown to the Spaniards. They had few advantages other than their own unscrupulousness and the fact that their motives were entirely unknown to their enemies.

After a harsh trek up into the heights of the Andes, Pizarro and his men reached the city of Cajamarca, mostly abandoned because of the civil war. Throughout their traversal, they were watched by the Inca's spies, and given their vulnerability, it is surprising that they were not ambushed and slaughtered by their numerically superior adversaries. Instead, they established themselves in Cajamarca and sent messengers to the nearby encampment where Atahualpa was currently staying, and persuaded him to meet with Pizarro and the other Spaniards in Cajamarca. Little is known about his motives, but one can assume that, confident after his victory over his brother and unimpressed by the small ragtag band of foreigners, it simply did not occur to him that they represented a serious threat to his power.

Whatever the case, when he arrived in Cajamarca, he came with a force of about 6,000 men, accompanied by a large contingent of nobles. These men were equipped with stone-age weapons such as wooden clubs and obsidian bladed spears. In the central square of Cajamarca, Atahualpa found only a few Spaniards, which made him feel perfectly safe about leading his entire retinue in. He could not know that Pizarro's hundred or so men were concealed in some of the building surrounding the square heavily armed and ready to attack.

What occurred next has been a matter of debate among historians for some time, but the essential facts seem to be the following. Vicente de Valverde, a priest who was accompanying Pizarro's expedition, emerged into the square with the interpreter Felipillo and read out the *requerimiento*, a document that demanded submission to the authority of the Pope and the king of Spain. Failure to submit to the terms of the *requerimiento* was regarded, in the legal apparatus the Spanish government had created to justify and legitimize conquest, as sufficient grounds for waging a "just war" against a non-Christian people. Having recited this strange document to Atahualpa, Valverde placed an equally strange document in his hand: a Catholic breviary. Not only could Atahualpa of course not read it, he had never even seen a book before. Puzzled by the gesture, he peered at the object for a moment, and then dropped it on the ground. Valverde declared to the Spaniards in hiding that the heathen had rejected the true faith, which gave them *carte blanche* for an attack. A round of cannon and musket fire burst out onto the square from the surrounding buildings, and a contingent of Spaniards on horseback made their way into the assembly of Indians, hacking at them with swords. The goal was to take the Inca emperor captive, and to do this they hacked off the arms of the private guards who carried his litter. The combat spilled out onto a surrounding plain, where a larger Inca army waited but failed to turn back the course of events. Those who did not fall to the Spaniards that evening fled back to their encampment.

Incredibly, Pizarro and his small force had managed to take the emperor captive and in the process slaughtered thousands of his soldiers. In truth, the Incas would never recover from the shock and trauma inflicted by this initial blow. Atahualpa, now their hostage, was apparently still unaware of their intention of total conquest of Peru, because he could have likely orchestrated his own rescue and the destruction of the invaders by summoning an overwhelmingly large army. Instead, he agreed to pay the ransom of an entire room filled with gold and two with silver, and he sent his emissaries to gather the necessary riches. He may have hoped that once they received the ransom, they would take the plunder back home and disturb him no more. In any case, while imprisoned by the Spaniards he arranged for his brother Huascar to be executed, suggesting that he was confident he would regain his position. This execution may have been a fatal move on his part, since it alienated many of the nobles of Cuzco and the southern provinces of the empire, most of whom had supported Huascar and would now be inclined to initially (and mistakenly) regard the Spaniards as liberators.

Meanwhile, the arrival of Almagro with over a hundred men created a restlessness among the Spaniards in Cajamarca, who wished to proceed toward the capital of Cuzco in search of more booty. Once the ransom was gathered, the Spaniards hesitated about what to do. It had been partly a delaying tactic, and now Atahualpa had less value to them alive. Since they intended to conquer his entire territory, they were obviously not going to allow him to return to his throne in Cuzco. Thus, in a move that proved controversial even at the time, Pizarro ordered the emperor's execution, hypocritically claiming on trumped up charges that Atahualpa had murdered his brother, practiced idolatry and attempted to revolt against the Spanish. Pizarro condemned him first to be baptized, then strangled and incinerated. This was particularly galling to the Inca, who believed that the burning of their bodies or corpses would prevent them from entering the afterlife.

Portrait depicting the death of Atahualpa, the last Sapa Inca.

Upon hearing the news of the Inca leader's death, Charles V wrote to Pizarro: "We have been displeased by the death of Atahualpa, since he was a monarch, and particularly as it was done in the name of justice." No European monarch appreciated the precedent established by regicide, even if it took place an ocean away. Nevertheless, while the execution of Atahualpa would prove a questionable action as far as the legitimacy of the conquest was concerned for the king of Spain and others, for the moment it allowed the Spaniards to fill the leadership vacuum in Peru in a way that would be favorable to their own situation. Trying to earn the trust of the Huascar faction in Cuzco, they arranged fro Huascar's brother, Tupac Hualpa, to ascend to the throne. The plan to be treated as allies and liberators in Cuzco did not ease their transit to the Inca capital. In the harsh and cold terrain between Cajamarca and Cuzco, they were repeatedly beset by armies loyal to Atahualpa, which managed to inflict significant casualties on them.

Pizarro and his ragged and exhausted army of conquistadors arrived in Cuzco in the middle of November 1533, almost a year after the massacre in Cajamarca. They were amazed by what they saw, and Pizarro reported back to the Spanish king, "This city is the greatest and the finest ever seen in this country or anywhere in the Indies... We can assure your Majesty that it is so beautiful and has such fine buildings that it would be remarkable even in Spain."

Unsurprisingly, it did not take the newcomers very long to lose whatever good will may have been directed at them by the partisans of Huascar, since they immediately set about looting gold and other valuables and treating the inhabitants with contempt and brutality. A new emperor had been appointed, Manco Inca, whom the Spaniards viewed as a puppet who would allow them to rule from behind the scenes. Manco, however, had his own agenda, and probably thought that once the Spaniards had exhausted the available riches they would move on.

16th century drawing by Guaman Poma depicting Manco Inca Yupanqui

Meanwhile, other conflicts emerged. Some native groups became allies of the Spanish, while others bided their time, waiting to drive out the invaders. And the northern provinces, generally loyal to Atahualpa, still needed to be brought under control. Almagro and Sebastián de Benalcázar set out to do just that, but once they had arrived in the region of Quito, they found themselves facing off with another Spaniard, Cortés's former lieutenant Pedro de Alvarado, who had set out on his own conquest mission from the northern Colombian coast. A battle nearly erupted between the two Spanish armies, but in the end Alvarado was successfully bribed with a share of Atahualpa's ransom.

Pedro de Alvarado

By now, however, a second and more deadly intra-Spanish conflict was afoot. Almagro, who had arrived late to Cajamarca, felt marginalized by the power of Pizarro and his brothers, particularly since he had never received a share of Atahualpa's ransom. He and his men believed that they had not yet enjoyed the promised fruits of conquest, even though their support had been crucial in the march to Cuzco. Through slow communication with Spain, it was established that the king had granted Pizarro jurisdiction over the north of the Inca empire and Almagro control over the south. It was unclear, though, which of them would obtain control over the all-important city of Cuzco, since the city lay at the dead center of Inca territory (its name translates as "the navel").

The attempts to defray the conflict probably exacerbated it. Judging that Cuzco was too far inland to serve as the Spanish capital, Pizarro founded and settled in the new city of Lima on a stretch of coast under his own control, which would assure his own importance and give him easier access to supplies and reinforcements from Panama. Meanwhile, Almagro set out on an expedition to conquer the territories to the south, obviously hoping to find territories even wealthier than the Inca heartland. He and his men were not prepared for the arid wasteland of the Atacama Desert that stretches between Peru and what is now Chile, and their two-year expedition brought much suffering and death to the Spaniards themselves and the natives they met, with no new wealth to show for it.

While the *almagristas*, as they were called, struggled across the Atacama, Pizarro put two of his younger brothers in charge of Cuzco so as to ensconce himself firmly in Lima. Gonzalo and Juan Pizarro were, unsurprisingly, disastrous governors who essentially gave free rein to the Spaniards to plunder, enslave, and rape. The alliances forged on the basis of the execution of Atahualpa were soon dissolved, and the young emperor Manco now decided to take matters into his own hands. The invaders in Cuzco still only numbered about 200, and they seemed distracted enough by their pillage to appear. Manco raised up an army of thousands, and in 1536 his forces laid siege to both Cuzco and Lima. Pizarro sent a desperate request for reinforcements from Panama, but the decisive support came in the form of the Almagro party, which arrived back in Cuzco in the Spring of 1537 and successfully drove away Manco and the Inca army.

While this sounds at first blush like a reversal of the tensions between Almagro and Pizarro, it was anything but. This was not a gesture of Spanish unity, it was an act of conquest. Almagro and his men took control of Cuzco, which they believed was theirs by right, and took the Pizarro brothers prisoner.

Meanwhile, the war with Manco was still not over. The Inca emperor had been driven away but not defeated, and he would return to give the Spaniards trouble for some years to come. But the central conflict that now consumed Peru was the one between Pizarro and Almagro, a conflict whose origins began before Pizarro's conquest of the Incas had even begun.

Almagro, embittered and furious, was determined to keep Cuzco, and in order to establish his claim he set out to Lima to take on his former business partner. Meanwhile, more Spaniards were arriving from Panama and beyond, desperate to get their hands on some of the land's abundant gold. The new colony was on the verge of descending into chaos, and Pizarro was determined to establish a persuasive and lasting hold on power. This made him reluctant to negotiate with Almagro, especially after the affront of the latter's arrest of his brothers in Cuzco. A series of battles between supporters of Pizarro and Almagro followed, even as Manco began to gather forces for a new attack.

Pizarro's most military capable brother, Hernando, finally defeated Almagro and his followers at Las Salinas in April of 1538, after which he dragged Almagro back to Cuzco. Almagro was tried, imprisoned, and ultimately garrotted in prison. His body was displayed in Cuzco's central square as a warning to his followers.

If the killing of Atahualpa was controversial, the execution of Almagro was even more so. While it removed the leader of resistance against Pizarro's power, it strengthened the resolve against Pizarro. It was also regarded as a treacherous and criminal power grab when word of the latest developments arrived to the Spanish crown. When Hernando Pizarro went back to Spain in 1539, he was immediately imprisoned.

With Almagro's death, Pizarro had ostensibly consolidated power in Peru, but the reality was far more complex. At this point, a relatively large contingent of natives were siding with the Spaniards, such that in the pivotal battle of Ollantaytambo between Hernando Pizarro and Manco Inca, Pizarro had tens of thousands of indigenous allies under his command. Likewise, many Inca nobles in Cuzco had essentially capitulated to Spanish rule and tried to make the best of the new power arrangements. On the other hand, Manco was still attempting to reestablish his own power base. Eventually, he gave up on retaking Cuzco and led a large group of nobles and other natives loyal to him down the eastern slope of the Andes and into the jungle, where he established a kind of second Inca capital in exile. The city of Vilcabamba, as it was called, held out for several decades more, although Manco himself was murdered in 1544 by *almagrista* renegades to whom he had unwisely given refuge. In the meantime, Manco's brother Paullu Inca served as a puppet for the Spanish in Cuzco, ultimately accepting baptism under the name Cristóval and providing military support to both Almagro and the Pizarros on different occasions.

Even after Diego de Almagro's death, his supporters, led by his son Diego, continued to chafe under the rule of the Pizarros. Between them, Manco Inca's forces and the almagrista faction constituted two separate power bases that rendered Francisco Pizarro's position as governor and captain general of Peru highly vulnerable.

Chapter 8: Pizarro's Death and the Aftermath

With Almagro dead and Manco in the distant jungle, Pizarro was at the height of his power and worldly success. By the end of the momentous decade of the 1530s, he was probably at least 65 and possibly near 70 years old, but he would not have the opportunity to enjoy his triumphs in peace in his later years. Instead, the man who rose to prominence by violence and treachery met a harsh but somewhat fitting end on June 26, 1541.

On that date, a group of about 20 conspirators under the leadership of the younger Diego de Almagro, who sought to avenge his father, broke into the governor's palace in Lima. The heavily armed attackers induced most of the palace guests to flee, while a handful stayed to fight. Even in his advanced age, Pizarro quickly tried to strap on his own breastplate and allegedly managed to kill a few of his attackers until the group started brutally stabbing him with swords. According to legend, Pizarro fell to the ground, formed a cross in his own blood and began praying. One of Spain's most notorious conquistadors was dead, and the conspirators proclaimed the young Almagro governor of Peru.

By the time of his death, Pizarro was not the most beloved leader to say the least. But he had just been murdered by the illegitimate offspring of Diego de Almagro and his indigenous mistress. Not surprisingly, the mestizo younger Almagro was not able to hold onto power for long. He would be dead within a year after Pizarro loyalists and reinforcements from Spain defeated him and the *almagristas* at the battle of Chupas in 1542. The younger Almagro was captured and executed.

After his death, Pizarro continued to cast a long shadow over events in Peru and beyond for some time. Even as new settlers flooded in and royal administrators attempted to rein in the excesses of the colonists, members of Pizarro's family and of his original cohort of conquistadors continued to be protagonists in the violent conflicts that continued to consume the new colony for decades. His brother Gonzalo, in particular, was probably the foremost figure among the original generation of conquistadors for the entire decade of the 1540s. Before Francisco's death, Gonzalo was appointed governor of Quito, and from there he set out to the east, descending from the Andes into the Amazon basin along with the explorer Francisco de Orellana. The expedition became one of the most notoriously disastrous in the history of New World exploration, with its initial contingent of several hundred Spaniards and Indian porters suffering 50% casualties as a result of desertion, death by disease, hostile Indian attacks, and general harsh conditions. Nevertheless, Orellana ultimately became the first European to navigate the entire course of the Amazon River. His reports of warlike women on the shores of the great river were the inspiration of the name given to the river and the great basin it flows through.

Gonzalo, however, had left Orellana's expedition before it had reached the Amazon and returned to Quito. It was there that he learned of his brother's death at the hands of Almagro and his supporters, but he did not arrive in Lima in time to participate in the final routing of his family's great rivals. If he hoped that the defeat of the *almagristas* would put the Pizarro family back in charge of Peru, he was soon proven wrong. The crown, appalled by the infighting, chaos, and brutality that had consumed Peru since the conquest, had decided to impose a much greater centralized control and had shipped out a fleet of royal administrators and bureaucrats to do so.

This development was not unique to Peru. In general, the Spanish crown had grown tired of the way that the conquistadors had treated their conquered lands as personal fiefdoms and failed to show due deference to their monarchical overseers. Throughout Europe, moreover, this was a period of centralization in which the monarchy was consolidating its hold on power by reining in the traditional privileges of the aristocracy. The conquistadors, mostly of humble backgrounds, had set out to the New World in order to ascend to the coveted status of landed gentry. Now the entire existence of such a class was threatened by new regulation, and the dreams of men like Pizarro would become increasingly impossible to realize under the new system. The successful and powerful men of new imperial territories like Peru would from now on mainly consist of bureaucratic strivers, lawyers and clergymen who respected hierarchy and the chain of command in a way that the original settlers never had. In Pizarro's capital of Lima, this new form of authority would arrive in the person of Blasco Núñez Vela, the royally appointed first viceroy of Peru.

Blasco Núñez Vela

There were other over-arching developments that led to further conflict between the new viceroy and Gonzalo Pizarro, who saw himself as his brother's legitimate successor. One of Núñez Vela's orders was to enforce the recently passed New Laws, a surprisingly humanitarian piece of legislation that attempted to protect the indigenous peoples of the New World from Spanish oppression. It is likely that the brutality of the Pizarros in Peru toward Atahualpa and his people played a role in winning over King Charles V to sign the new laws. They were also the result of the tireless campaigning of the Dominican friar Bartolomé de las Casas, who attacked the cruelty and rapacity of the Spanish conquistadors in unforgiving terms in a series of books, pamphlets, sermons, and public debates.

The New Laws aimed above all to reform the institution of the *encomienda*, which had played an important role in the conquest since Columbus's earliest settlements. Soldiers who participated in any conquest of new territory would be granted an *encomienda*, which was an "entrustment" of land with a certain number of natives whose labor they would be able to exploit by demanding tribute in exchange for instruction in Christianity. It was an essentially feudal arrangement, and it had led to the creation of *de facto* slavery throughout the colonies. The New Laws attempted to make indigenous peoples into free wage laborers and to significantly curtail the power of the *encomenderos*. It is debatable how much of the crown's motivation was humanitarian and how much the enforcement of natives' rights provided a convenient pretext for curtailing the disruptive power of the conquistadors and centralizing control over overseas territories, but the immediate results were more dramatic in their impact on the attitudes and loyalties of the Spanish colonists than on the lot of the natives.

The New Laws were only selectively enforced in the end, but their initial introduction to Peru was a scandal to all the original settlers who regarded themselves as having earned their power and positions through their military service. Making matters worse, Núñez arrived with orders to confiscate the property of anyone who had been directly involved in the feud between Pizarro and Almagro. Gonzalo Pizarro managed to unite most of the Spanish settlers in a rebellion against the New Laws and the viceroy, and he and in his supporters managed to kill Núñez in battle in 1546. At this point, Pizarro became unofficial ruler of Peru, and in a remarkable turn of events he and his followers decided to declare Peru an independent territory no longer under the rule of the King of Spain. Even more audaciously, Gonzalo named himself king of Peru, claiming that the Incas had legitimately abdicated power to his brother and he was the rightful successor. This was a remarkable turn of events given that Peru would not again seek independence for more than 250 years.

In 1547, a royal army arrived from Spain along with Pedro de la Gasca, who had been appointed as Núñez's replacement. De la Gasca shrewdly promised not to enforce the most onerous of the new laws, thus persuading a large contingent of colonists to withdraw their support from Gonzalo Pizarro's outlandish coup. Now the Spanish forces controlled Lima while Pizarro took refuge in Cuzco, where he had some loyalty among the colonists, veterans of his brother's campaigns, and some of the surviving Inca nobility who had intermarried with the conquistadors. But his base of support was small and dwindling now that the New Laws were less of a concern, and his forces were finally routed at the old Incan fortress of Sacsayhuamán, outside of Cuzco. He was beheaded by the victorious Spanish force. With his death in April 1548, the Pizarro family's hold on Peru was definitively broken, and the process of viceregal centralization had succeeded.

Pedro de la Gasca

The defiant faction of Incas at the Amazonian stronghold of Vilcabamba held out considerably longer in their bid for independence from Spanish control. After Manco Inca's murder, Manco's son Sayri Tupac succeeded him and ruled for over ten years until finally returning to Cuzco and submitting to the new order. His brother Titu Cusi took over and remained in power until 1571, trying to maintain friendly relations with the Spaniards and even accepting Christian baptism. After his death, he was succeeded by his younger brother Tupac Amaru.

Around the same time, two Spanish emissaries were killed in the jungle near Vilcabamba, and this gave the viceroy, Francisco de Toledo, the pretext he needed to declare war against the troublesome enclave of holdouts. He sent an expeditionary force into the difficult jungle terrain and, despite difficulties, they drove Tupac Amaru out of Vilcabamba and captured him and much of his entourage, along with the remains of the two previous emperors and several sacred objects. The latter were taken to Cuzco and burned as idols and as a warning to any sympathizers among the surviving natives. Tupac Amaru, like Gonzalo Pizarro, was beheaded. As with the executions of Atahualpa and Diego de Almagro, the punishment was controversial: priests, administrators, and finally the Spanish king himself all objected to Toledo's act. But it was done, and now the last vestige of the Inca power structure was gone. It is a surprising and little-known fact that, despite the apparently decisive blow dealt to the Incas by Pizarro's murder of Atahualpa, the Inca state had remained in existence in modified form for nearly 40 years afterwards.

The Dominican friar Bartolomé de Las Casas (c. 1484-1566), who had first-hand experience witnessing the actions of the Spanish conquistadors, damned Pizarro for his cruelty in destroying the Inca Empire. In his *Short Account of the Destruction of the Indies,* written in 1542, Las Casas described Pizarro's violent rampage in search of gold, writing that he "criminally murdered and plundered his way through the region, razing towns and cities to the ground and slaughtering and otherwise tormenting in the most barbaric fashion imaginable the people who lived there." As evidence of the crimes, Las Casas quoted an affidavit sworn by the Franciscan Brother Marcos de Niza, who was present during Pizarro's conquest. Among many atrocities Brother Marcos wrote, "I testify that I saw with my own eyes Spaniards cutting off the hands, noses and ears of local people, both men and women, simply for the fun of it."

Peru would go onto become the wealthiest of Spain's colonies, with the inhabitants of Lima living in legendary opulence even as the wealth was built on the back of impoverished Indian labor that was usually difficult to distinguish from slavery. The New Laws remained largely unenforced, and the harsh treatment of the Indians employed in agriculture and mining led to a number of rebellions. The first that truly shook Spain's hold on power was led by a man who assumed the title of Tupac Amaru II. Even after Peru gained independence from Spain in 1824, the highly unequal political and economic system first created by Pizarro remained largely intact. The capital of Lima remained the center of power, with much of its wealthy and middle class of Spanish or other European stock, while the vast indigenous majority remained in the Andean mountains, living in practically feudal conditions.

Only in recent years, especially with mass migration of indigenous people from the countryside into the large cities, has the traditional power structure begun to shift somewhat, a development perhaps most clearly signaled by the election of Peru's first indigenous president, Alejandro Toledo, in 2001. Francisco Pizarro's most significant ongoing legacy, much like his most significant immediate legacy, is a conflict over power and resources. This conflict will continue to consume Peru and the other countries built on former Inca territories (Ecuador, Bolivia) until the inequalities first put in place by the conquistadors and perpetuated by the Spanish colonial governments have been resolved.

Compared to other notables of what has come to be known as the Age of Exploration, Francisco Pizarro enjoys a less than assured reputation. His relative neglect is somewhat surprising in a number of ways, but it can probably be explained on the basis of several factors. If judged purely on the basis of what many of his contemporaries sought in the period of his activity – adventure, military triumph, land, and wealth – Pizarro probably outstrips all of them. After all, Christopher Columbus, who has a country named after him and whose deeds are celebrated on holidays in dozens of countries, never even set out to discover previously unknown lands: he wished to reach Asia and tap into the lucrative Indian Ocean spice trade. He not only failed in this endeavor but ended up being expelled from the one colony he did found (Hispaniola), and he never reached a land abundant with the kind of resources he expected. Hernán Cortés subdued the powerful and wealthy Aztec empire, but his reign as governor of the new Spanish colony he founded was short and controversial. While he remained relatively wealthy, he died embittered, like Columbus, from a sense of not being appreciated by the powers whose interests he had served. Ferdinand Magellan succeeded where Columbus had failed: he reached Asia by a westward route, giving the Portuguese crown privileged access to the spice and silk trades. But even though he is (ironically) remembered as the man who circumnavigated the globe, Magellan died in the Philippines during his famous journey, thus unable to enjoy any glory.

Pizarro's last years and death were certainly as fraught as those of the contemporaries just named – he was ultimately murdered by mutinous Spaniards drawn from among his own former comrades in arms – but his military achievements were if anything more remarkable than those of Cortés, at least in so far as the empire he overthrew was larger, wealthier, and better prepared in military terms. By establishing a foothold on the central ridge of the Andes, he also opened up immense new territories for Spanish imperial expansion, which would soon encompass most of the South American continent. The Spanish presence in Mexico, in contrast, did not lead to a massive expansion into North America on the same scale. Lima, the city Pizarro founded on the coast of Peru in 1535, would go on to become one of the wealthiest cities in the world for a time, on the strength of the unimaginably vast silver and gold deposits of the Andes. Even more than the precious metals of Mexico, the wealth of Peru exploited by Pizarro and his successors would have a dramatic and lasting impact on the global economy, and arguably it was a primary impetus for the growth of modern European capitalism

Although they were distantly related through Cortés's mother, Doña Catalina Pizarro, Francisco Pizarro was of a lower social rank than Cortés, who came from modest means but possessed a legitimately aristocratic lineage on both sides. An illegitimate child, he had been a humble swineherd before setting off to the Indies in the hope of bettering his lot. Perhaps even more significantly, Pizarro possessed little education and was either illiterate or barely literate. Cortés, in contrast, had attended the prestigious University of Salamanca and, as a trained notary and magistrate, was a sophisticated rhetorician whose finely phrased letters to the monarchy won him support and admiration, not least from the historian Francisco López de Gómara, who wrote a glowing biography of the conqueror of Mexico. To put it differently, while Cortés and Pizarro did much the same thing, the former did so with greater literary flourish, and the result has been a lasting aura of heroism and boldness that has eluded the latter. Finally, Pizarro died even more ignominiously than Cortés or Columbus, having overseen the descent of his new Spanish colony into a vicious civil war and been murdered by the son of his former business partner.

In truth, and especially from a 21st century vantage point, it is hard to find much to admire in either Cortés or Pizarro. Both were venal, conniving, and brutal; both achieved much of what they accomplished through a combination of treachery and callous disregard for human life; both have on their hands the practical destruction of an entire civilization. Not surprisingly, in modern Peru, Pizarro is not even remotely a national hero. For perhaps the majority of the Peruvian population, descended partly or fully from the indigenous groups he and the other Spanish conquerors subjugated and essentially enslaved, he is regarded as an invader and an illegitimate ruler whose actions set the country on a catastrophic path. And indeed, the inequalities of the colonial order he established, in which the indigenous people became largely subservient to the Spanish conquerors, still remain a fact of life: most of Peru's wealthiest citizens are of European descent, while its poorest people are almost universally of indigenous background. In the capital city of Lima, popular repudiation recently forced the government to move an equestrian statue of Pizarro away from the central plaza and to a less central location. Like the other conquistadors, Pizarro's legacy has declined even moreso since 1992, the quincentennial of Columbus's landfall in the Indies. In addition to helping Columbus retain the spotlight, that year's commemoration was a watershed moment for alternative versions of history, in which the experiences of the native peoples who experienced the consequences of Spanish aggression and greed took precedence over traditional narratives of conquering heroes. It can be safely assumed that Native American perception of Pizarro will not improve anytime soon.

Chapter 9: The Survival of the Inca

As one would expect from a great and powerful civilization, many aspects of the Inca culture survived the depredations of the Spanish. The revolt of Manco Inca immediately after the Spanish occupation of Cuzco was not the last of Inca uprisings. In the 18th century, John Santos Atahualpa, who claimed descent from the Inca ruler murdered by the Spanish more than a century before, assembled a large force of warriors and overthrew Spanish authority in the jungles of Peru, establishing an independent territory from which the Franciscans were expelled. Eventually the Spanish managed to re-establish control over the secessionist territory.

Another bloody revolt led by Túpac Amaru II in the 18th century was put down with great difficulty by the Spanish army. Túpac Amaru II was taken with his family to Cuzco in 1780 where, after being forced to witness the execution of his wife and members of his family, he was taken to the main plaza and cruelly tortured and beheaded, with his body also being quartered. Túpac Amaru's followers abandoned the two cities they had begun to build in the Vilcabamba Valley and fled into the jungle. There are tales that somewhere in the jungle of Peru or Bolivia the last of the Incas, called the Quechuans by some, built a city called Paititi where they hid a great store of gold. To this day adventurers, inspired by New Age beliefs, continue to search for the lost last Inca city and its hoard of gold. After Túpac Amaru's revolt the Spanish banned the use of Quechua that they had used as a vehicle for the political and religious transformation of Inca culture, yet another attempt at eradicating a culture that was proving far too hard for the Spanish to kill.

Túpac Amaru II

From the beginnings of Spanish domination in the region up until the present day, the culture of the Incas survived in one form or another. It is a testament to the strength of generations of Incas that despite the slaughter of members of the elite, the destruction and reuse of the Inca city of Cuzco (including the building of the Cathedral of Santo Domingo over an Inca temple), the intense efforts to stamp out Inca religion, and the decimation of the Inca population through disease and forced labor, the Spanish did not succeed in permanently abolishing the independent culture of native Peruvians.

Peruvian Banknote with Portrait of Garcilaso de la Vega's, 1970's

Much of what we know about the details of Inca life before and after the conquest was recorded by Garcilaso de la Vega (1539-1616) in his *Comentarios Reales de los Incas*, published in Lisbon in 1609. De la Vega was the son of a conquistador and Isabel Suarez Chimpu Ocllo, an Inca princess who was the daughter of Tupac Inca Yupanqui. How de la Vega described Inca culture was colored by his education in Spanish so that the oral traditions of his ancestors on his mother's side are recorded from the perspective of a European. This combination of Inca and Spanish traditions and customs was paralleled by the development of a religious syncretism in which Inca practices and beliefs were fused with Christian precepts.

An interesting document prepared by a notary for Juan Sicos Inca in 1632 to verify his noble heritage, and thus render him immune from being forced to labor (mit'a) for the Spanish, records a religious procession that he led through the streets of Cuzco while carrying the standard of the Virgin. Juan Sicos' costume for the parade was a combination of traditional Inca garb - strings of pearls and precious stones and two chains of gold - and the festive costume of a Spanish hidalgo - armour, a sword and dagger. Following the standard of the Virgin in the parade was a second one held by three natives dressed in the "ancient style". The iconography of the standard, a canvas painted on both sides, was entirely Inca. The combination of Christian and Inca religion continues to this day.

Not only did the Inca culture survive in a modified form in Peru, but their culture also became an important part of the mentality of Europeans in assimilating a culture that for some was much superior to their own sophisticated but flawed society. The fascination with the Incas, particularly with Inca elite and most particularly with elite females, is clear in the legends and literature of Europe. According to one tale, Sebastián Bérzeviczy, the owner of Niedzica Castle in southern Poland, went to Peru and fell in love with an Inca princess. The daughter of this union, Umina, married the nephew of the insurrectionist Inca Túpac Amaru II. This nephew inherited the sacred scrolls of the Incas, which are said to have eventually been brought to

Poland before they ultimately disappeared. Naturally, the scrolls were believed to contain details about the lost treasure of the Incas.

In France the Peruvian or Inca princess was given life by the popular writer Françoise de Graffigny in her 1747 novel *Letteres d'une Péruvienne*. In the story, the Inca princess Zilia, writing to her fiancé the Inca Aza, tells of her abduction from the Temple of the Sun by the Spanish, her rescue by French sailors and her subsequent observations of French society. De Graffigny's novel was exceedingly popular, and it was published into more than 140 editions in French and other languages over the next century. Madame De Graffigny said that she was inspired to begin research on her novel by reading Garcilaso de la Vega's book after attending a performance of Voltaire's play *Alzire*. First performed in Paris in 1736, Voltaire's play is the love story of the Inca princess Alzire. On one level Voltaire's play and De Graffigny's novel were popular because they dealt with an exotic culture that was fascinating for its abundance of gold and intermittent violence, and the French idealistically portrayed the Inca as a kind of utopian civilization. Indeed, European enthusiasm for a love story that takes place within the context of a clash of Spanish and Inca cultures has had a long life. Giuseppe Verdi composed an opera, *Alzira*, with a libretto based on Voltaire's play, which was first performed in Naples in 1845.

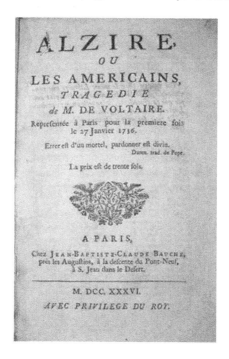

In Peru, Inca civilization has had a long life that is more prosaic than its manifestation in Europe. The declaration of independence of Peru from Spanish colonial authority in 1821 did not do much to improve the lot of the native population. In fact, the termination of the mit'a system of taxation which had continued under the Spanish and its replacement by a monetary system was detrimental to the condition of the Andean natives. Furthermore, the Inca system of land allocation without transfer of title - a kind of communal ownership of land - was replaced by systematic individual land tenure. The imposition of strict laws on the control of the land created the conditions that even today gives rise to often violent disputes with respect to mining operations. The bulk of the Andean population still struggles to maintain their culture in a system of governance that is quite foreign to them.

In the 1920's there arose a movement in Peru known as indegenismo, which sought to replace capitalist ideas of social organization with ancient Andean ones and revive the customs and traditions of the indigenous peoples. The coupling of Inca nationalism and its harkening back to a utopian world, one that has been interpreted by some intellectuals as being communal in nature, is a continuing motif in relations between the two cultures of Peru. The strongest current manifestation of indegenismo is the yearly celebration of Inti Raymi, which was revived in 1944, in which a dignitary dressed as an Inca king is paraded before a crowd of native Andeans and tourists. The ersatz Inca ruler addresses the crowd in Imperial Incan, a special form of Quechua that is still understood by some 2.5 million speakers of the language. The festival involves a number of actors and dancers following a script that was developed from the writings of Garcilaso de la Vega.

Pictures of Inti Raymi Festival (Festival of the Sun) at Sacsayhuaman, Cusco. Photos by Cyntia Motta

While the Incas in Peru continue to evolve into a society that can in some way serve to ameliorate the prejudices of history and ensure that the goals of indegenismo are considered in the evolution of the modern Peruvian state, the rest of the world remains entranced by real and imaginary tales of Inca gold and the story of the Spanish conquest. The success of Paul Shaffer's play *The Royal Hunt of the Sun*, performed in England in 1964 and subsequently on Broadway, is an example of this fascination. Schaffer's drama, which tells of Pizarro's greed and Atahualpa's agony, was made into a film in 1969, represented as an opera in 2006 and revived on the English stage in 2006.

Between the popular depictions of the Inca on both sides of the Atlantic, and the ongoing mystery over their great cities and ruins, one of the few things that can be said with certainty about the Inca is that their civilization and empire will continue to fascinate the world well into the future.

Printed in Great Britain
by Amazon

25328402R00036